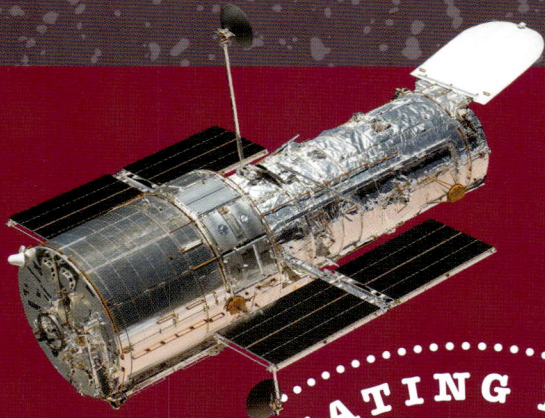

ENGINEERING

BY ANGIE SMIBERT

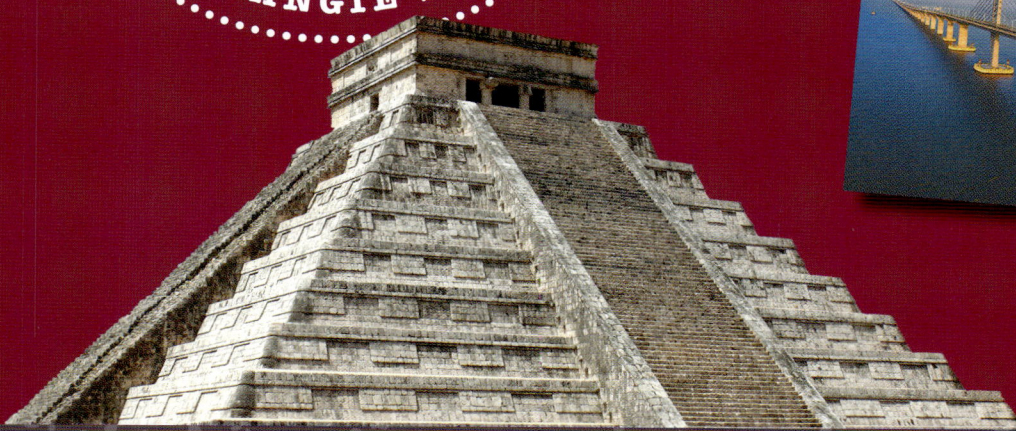

The Child's World®
childsworld.com

Published by The Child's World®
1980 Lookout Drive • Mankato, MN 56003-1705
800-599-READ • www.childsworld.com

Photographs ©: Lukiyanova Natalia Frenta/Shutterstock Images, cover (pyramid), 1 (pyramid), 7; Nick Poon/iStockphoto, cover (bridge), 1 (bridge), 13; Jon D. Patton/iStockphoto, cover (fighter jet), 1 (fighter jet), 18; Marcel Clemens/Shutterstock Images, cover (Hubble telescope), 1 (Hubble telescope), 21; Shutterstock Images, 3, 4, 5, 8, 9, 18–19, 20, 24, back cover (airplane); Hung Chung Chih/Shutterstock Images, 6; Sebastian Studio/Shutterstock Images, 10; Wan Cheuk Nang/Shutterstock Images, 11; Delpix Art/iStockphoto, 12, back cover (Palm Jumeirah); Massimo Parisi/Shutterstock Images, 14; Everett Historical/Shutterstock Images, 15; Wayne Starr/Express Newspapers/AP Images, 16; Robert Markowitz/JSC/NASA, 16–17

ISBN 9781503844612 (Reinforced Library Binding)
ISBN 9781503846241 (Portable Document Format)
ISBN 9781503847439 (Online Multi-user eBook)
LCCN 2019957696

Printed in the United States of America

ABOUT THE AUTHOR

Angie Smibert is the author of several young-adult and middle-grade science fiction and fantasy novels. She has also written more than two dozen educational titles just like this one. She was a science writer at NASA's Kennedy Space Center for many, many years. She received NASA's prestigious Silver Snoopy award as well as several other awards for her work.

CONTENTS

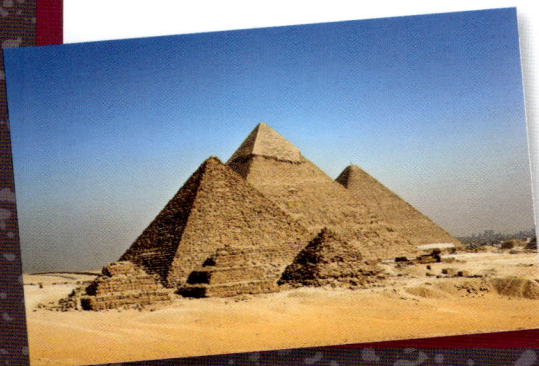

INTRODUCTION

Engineers are clever! They solve practical problems using science, technology, and math. They design and build structures and machines. And they have been doing so for thousands of years.

GREAT PYRAMIDS OF GIZA

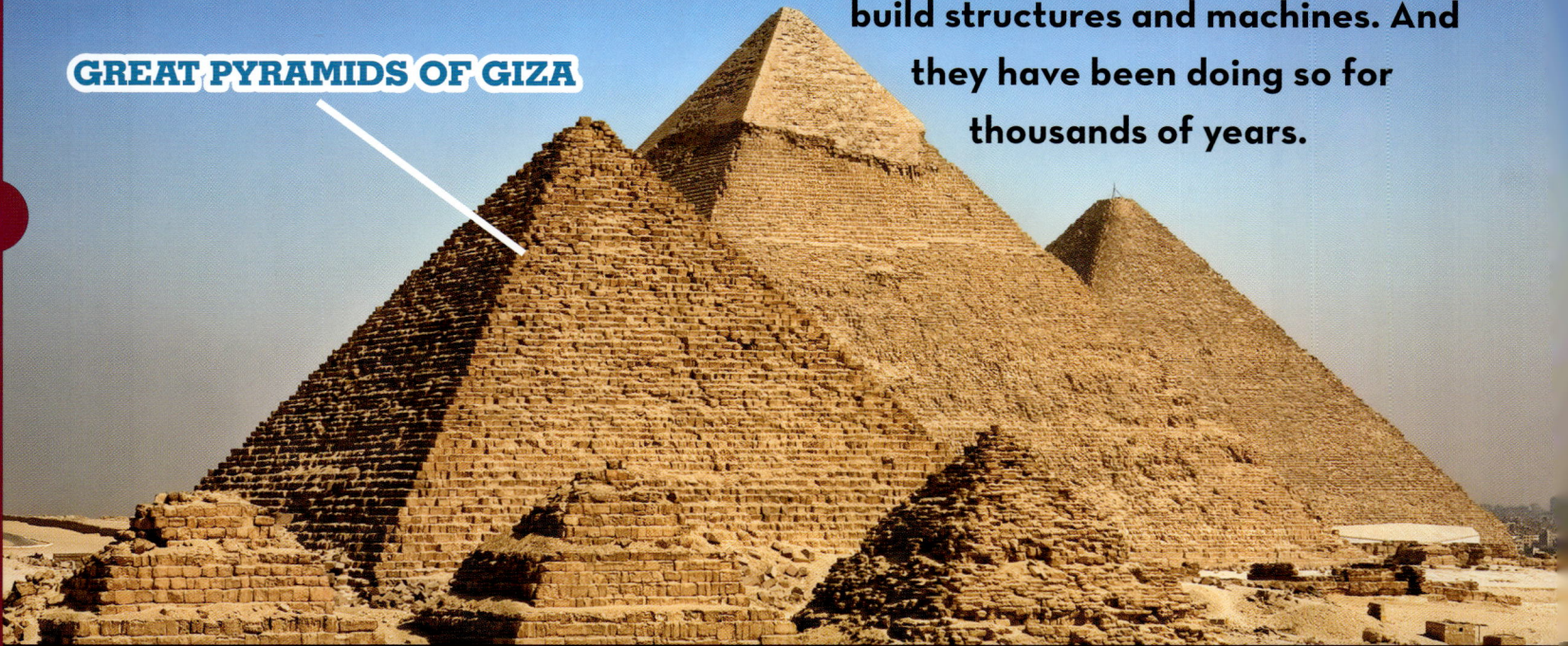

Ancient Egyptian and Maya engineers built pyramids. Ancient Chinese engineers built massive walls. Other ancient engineers built places of entertainment and worship.

THREE GORGES DAM

Today, engineers continue to build fantastic buildings, dams, and even islands. They create computers that can connect the world and robots that can go to outer space. Engineers make rockets that carry people to the moon. Their creations have even captured images beyond the solar system! Let's explore some of engineers' cleverest achievements.

CHAPTER ONE

Ancient Wonders

The Great Wall of China is 13,171 miles (21,197 km) long. It took centuries to build. Some bricks are held together with a mixture that includes sticky rice flour! Even today, weeds cannot grow between those bricks.

About one-third of the Great Wall ▶ has disappeared. The wall was built over a period of more than 2,000 years. Over time, about 1,219 miles (1,962 km) of the Great Wall have been lost. Weather is to blame for much of this loss. Wind and rain wore away the wall. But people have also stolen pieces of it. Locals have taken bricks to build villages and to sell to tourists.

3,800 years

▲

The Great Pyramid in Egypt was the tallest building on Earth for 3,800 years! The Great Pyramid was completed around 2560 BC. Scientists think the structure was originally 481 feet (147 m) high.

The Great Pyramid was made of 2.3 million blocks. The average weight of each block is 2.5 tons (2.3 metric tons). The ancient Egyptians did not have wheels or **pulleys** to help them move the stones. So how did they do it? One **theory** is that they pulled strong sleds over wet sand.

Twice a year, a snake-shaped shadow slithers down the stairs of Mexico's Pyramid of Kukulcán. Ancient engineers built it this way. That is because the pyramid is a temple to a snake god. It is part of the ancient Maya city Chichén Itzá.

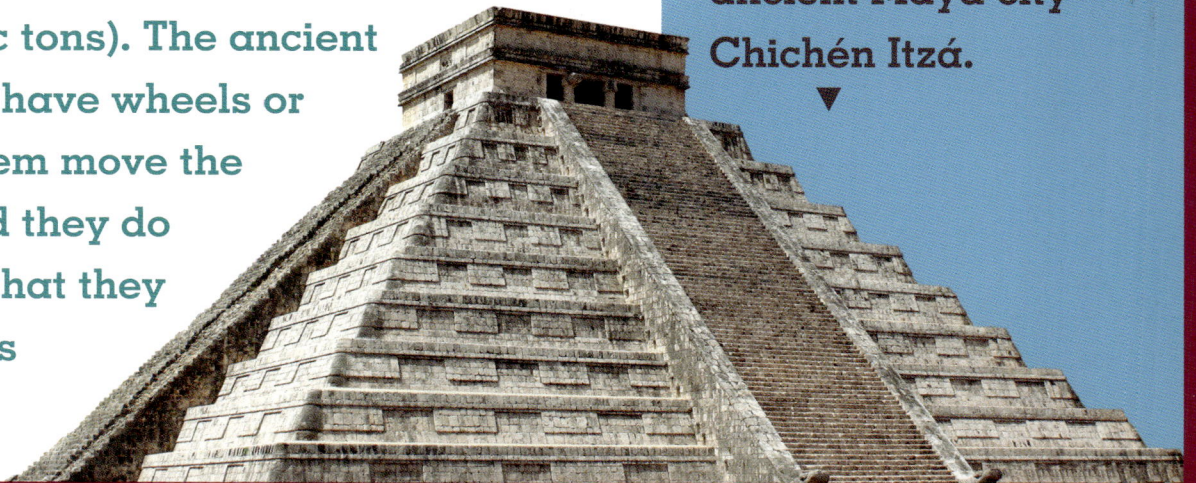

▼

Astounding Buildings

The Colosseum in Rome, Italy, could be flooded for naval battles. Romans built it from about AD 70 to 80 for races, festivals, and combat games. One of these games was a naval battle! The Romans flooded the Colosseum floor with water. Then **gladiators** on small ships fought. Crowds watched. Modern engineers are not sure how the Romans filled the arena with water. ▼

The Colosseum arena had 36 trap doors. The trap doors released wild animals during games. Underneath the arena, Roman engineers built a network of tunnels, shafts, and pens. Workers moved the animals through this network. Hoists lifted heavy animals, such as elephants, up to the arena's main level.

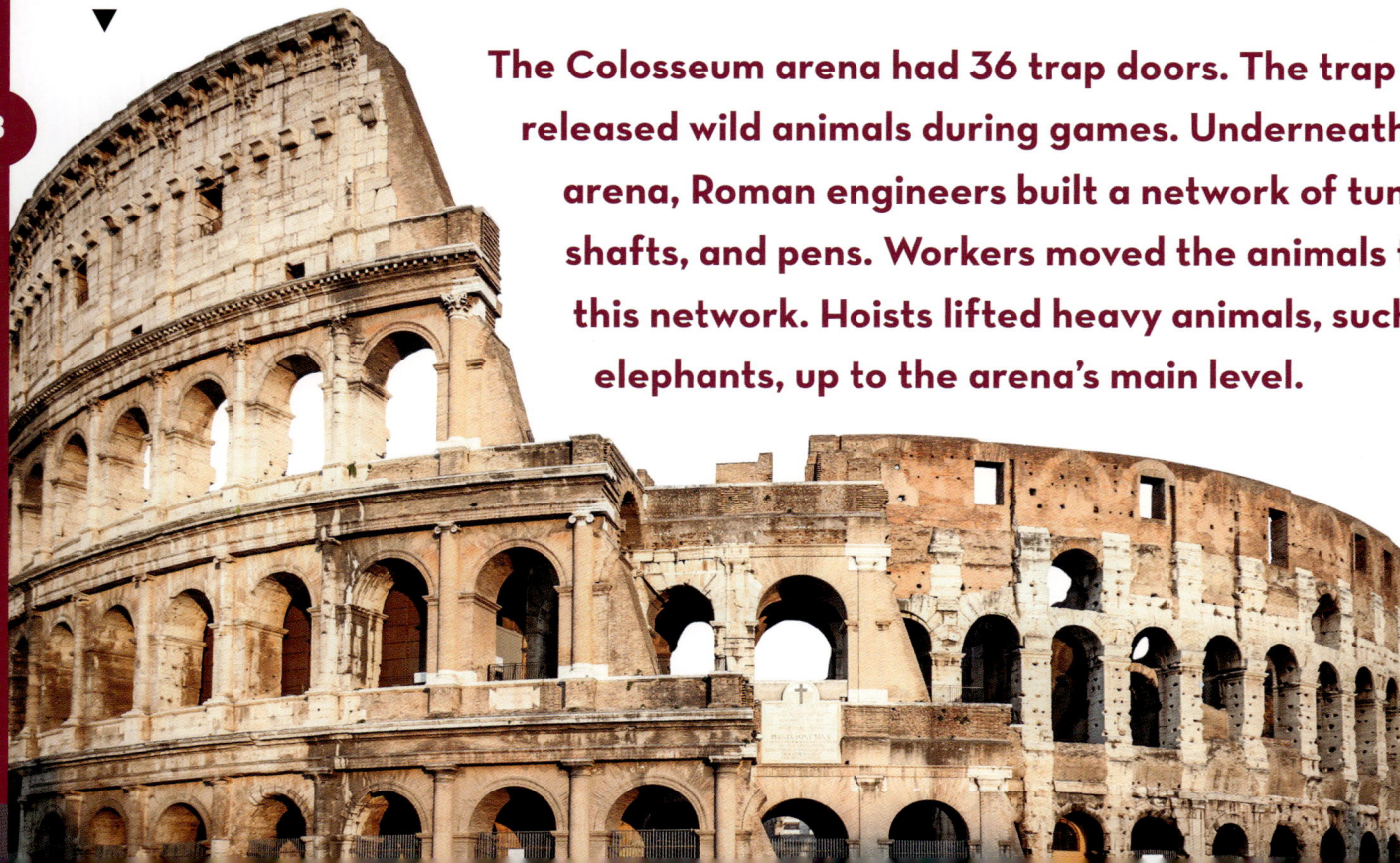

The Lalibela churches in Ethiopia were built from the top down! During the 12th century, workers carved down into solid rock to create 11 churches. All of the churches are below ground level. The largest is 35 feet (11 m) deep. ▶

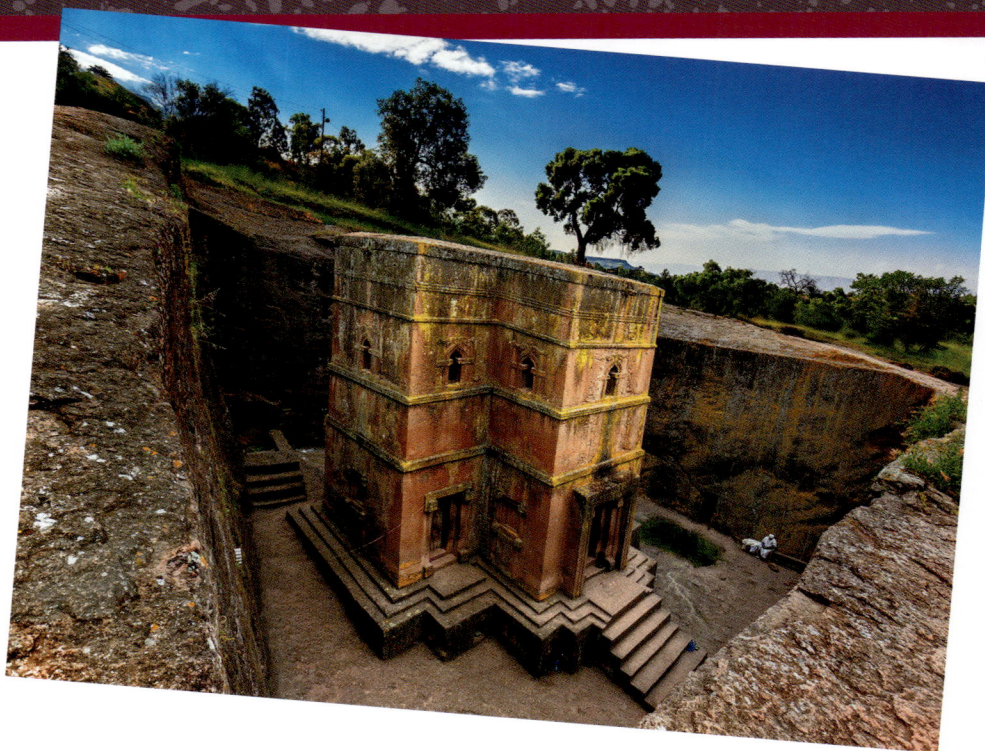

656 feet

◀ A giant moat around the Angkor Wat temple in Cambodia keeps the temple from sinking. The moat is 3 miles (5 km) around and 656 feet (200 m) wide. It was dug by about 5,000 workers. The moat keeps the **groundwater** level from rising or sinking. This supports the temple's **foundation**.

CHAPTER TWO

For the Record Books

10

Kingda Ka is the world's tallest roller coaster! Located at Six Flags Great Adventure in New Jersey, it is 456 feet (139 m) high at its tallest point. It is also the second-fastest roller coaster. The coaster can reach 128 miles per hour (206 kmh) in 3.5 seconds. The whole ride only lasts 59 seconds.

◄ Burj Khalifa is the tallest building in the world. It is located in Dubai, United Arab Emirates (UAE). This structure is 2,723 feet (830 m) tall. That is nearly twice the height of the Empire State Building.

The Bailong Elevator is the tallest outdoor lift. The Zhangjiajie National Forest in China is famous for its huge sandstone pillars. The Bailong Elevator takes visitors 1,070 feet (326 m) up the side of one of these pillars. ▶

France's Millau **Viaduct** is the tallest bridge in the world. One of its towers is 1,125 feet (343 m) tall. That is taller than the Eiffel Tower. Many engineers thought this bridge was impossible to build. Finished in 2004, the bridge stands 886 feet (270 m) above the Tarn River valley.

31.5 miles

▲

The Channel Tunnel is the longest underwater tunnel. It goes under the English Channel. It links England and France. It is 31.5 miles (50.7 km) long. Twenty-three and a half miles (37.8 km) of the tunnel are underwater. It took three years to dig from France to England. Some of the digging machines were as long as two football fields!

Longest and Largest

▲

The largest human-made island is shaped like a palm tree. The island is called Palm Jumeirah. It was built by the UAE. The outer part of the island slows down waves. The fronds have luxury houses. And the trunk has stores, apartments, and hotels.

The Three Gorges Dam in China is so big that it slowed Earth's rotation! The massive dam has about 988 million cubic feet (28 million cu. m) of concrete. It also needed more than 510,000 tons (463,000 metric tons) of steel. The dam flooded the Yangtze River for 375 miles (604 km). It created a **reservoir** that holds 42 billion tons (38 billion metric tons) of water. The weight of both the dam and the water slowed Earth by .06 microseconds!

42 billion tons

The world's longest sea bridge is 34 miles (55 km) long. The Hong Kong-Zhuhai-Macau Bridge stretches across the Pearl River delta in China. It connects Hong Kong and mainland China. The bridge is really three bridges, 4.2 miles (6.8 km) of tunnel, and several human-made islands.

CHAPTER THREE

Incredible Machines

The first computer was never fully built. In the 1820s, Charles Babbage built a machine to do complex math. But he never finished the machine because it was too expensive. If he had completed it, the computer would have used 25,000 parts. It also would have weighed 4 tons (3.6 metric tons).

Babbage designed other computers. A model of one is in the Science Museum in London. ▼

The first computer program was written for a computer that was never built. Ada Lovelace wrote the first program in 1843. She wrote out the steps to solve certain math problems. Lovelace is considered the first programmer.

The world's smallest computer is smaller than a grain of rice! In 2018, the University of Michigan created a computer that is .3 millimeters long.

To get to the moon, the *Apollo* spacecraft needed a computer. But in the 1960s, most computers were huge. Some were the size of refrigerators. And the *Apollo* would be small. Engineers shrank the *Apollo* computer to about 1 cubic foot (.03 cu. m). It was about the size of a briefcase.

One of the first computers was so big, you could park a bus in it! The ENIAC was completed in 1946. The computer filled a very large room at the University of Pennsylvania. It took up about 1,800 square feet (167 sq. m) of floor space.

Rad Robots

In 2020, a robotic arm and hand called LUKE was being tested. It is for people who have lost their arm. LUKE can be linked to a wearer's nerves. It can help the wearer feel objects in that limb again.

▲

Some people have worn exoskeletons. An exoskeleton is a robotic device. It fits over the legs and helps people walk. Claire Lomas is paralyzed from the chest down. In 2012, she finished the London Marathon in an exoskeleton. It took 17 days of walking.

There are robots swimming in an Italian lagoon! Engineers designed robots inspired by fish, mussels, and other sea life. The robots help scientists study the sea life and water in the lagoon.

Astronauts use a human-shaped robot called Robonaut 2 (R2). It does both dangerous and routine tasks. Astronauts control R2 with a laptop. R2's legs can be removed so that it can attach to workbenches or equipment. It also has climbing legs. These legs have seven joints and clamps for feet. R2 can climb around and then attach itself with its "feet" to do work!

◀

CHAPTER FOUR

Takeoff!

The largest plane is almost ► the size of a football field. The Russian *Antonov AN-225* was designed to carry a **space shuttle**. It is large enough to hold 50 cars!

50 cars

18

The SR-71 Blackbird holds the records for both the fastest and highest flights. In 1976, an SR-71 climbed to 85,069 feet (25,929 m). Most commercial airplanes only fly between 30,000 and 40,000 feet (9,140 and 12,190 m). In 1990, an SR-71 flew across the United States in 67 minutes. The jet reached an average speed of 2,125 miles per hour (3,419 kmh)!

SpaceX Falcon rockets can land themselves back on the ground. Most rockets are not reusable. After launch, most rockets fall into the ocean. But the SpaceX Falcon rockets and **boosters** can fly themselves back and set down vertically. Then they can be used again!

19

The *Saturn 5* rocket burned up more fuel in one second than a jumbo jet uses in one hour. During launch, the mighty *Saturn 5* gobbled up 20 tons (18 metric tons) of fuel per second. A large airplane burns about 10 tons (9 metric tons) of fuel per hour. The enormous rocket used this fuel to produce the 7.5 million pounds (3.4 million kg) of **thrust** needed to get itself off the ground.

20

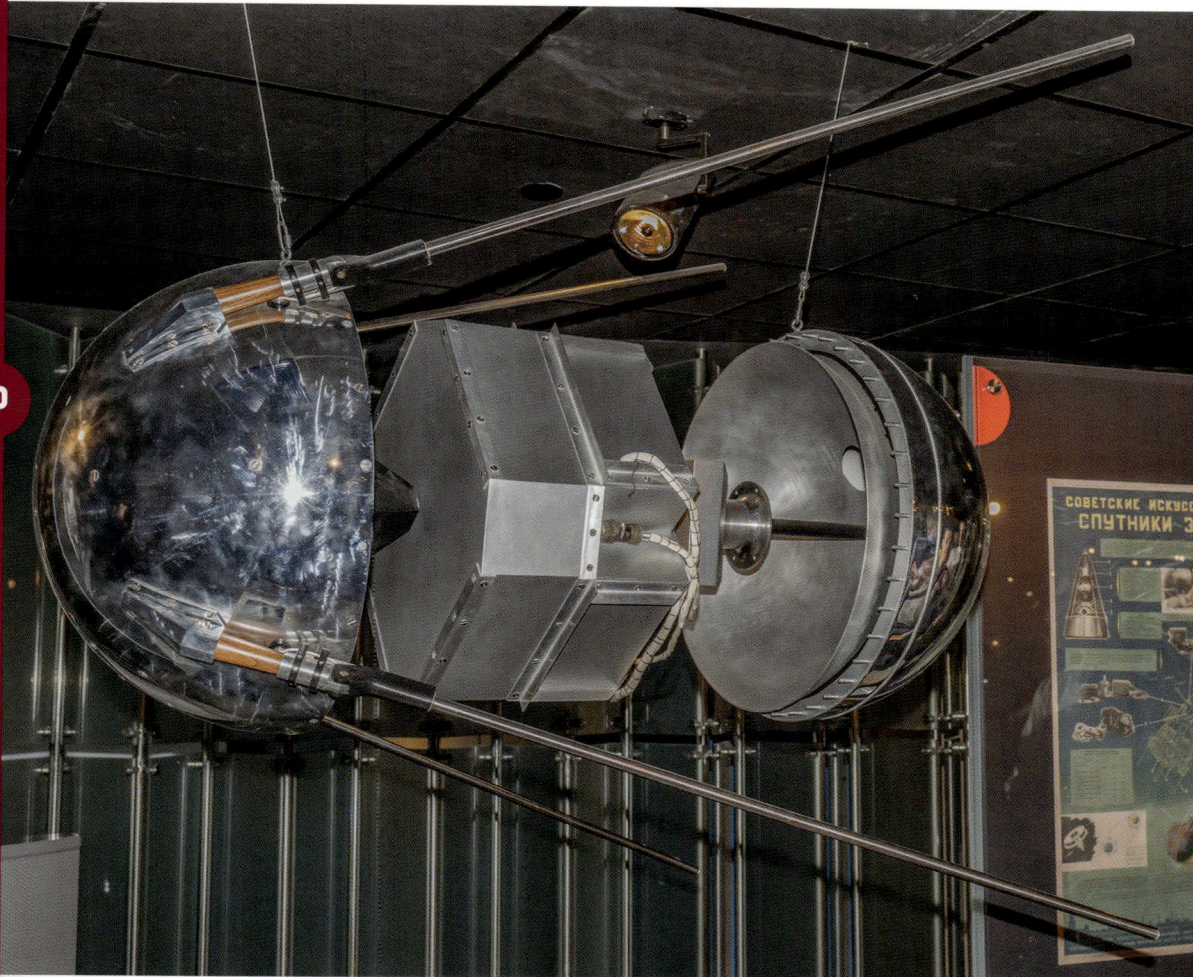

In 1957, the Soviet Union launched the first **satellite** into space. It was called *Sputnik 1*. It was about the size and shape of a beach ball! This design helped it get off the ground.

The Hubble Space Telescope's first pictures came back fuzzy. After Hubble launched in 1990, NASA discovered that one of the telescope's mirrors was flawed. Three years later, astronauts were able to fix it—while it **orbited** Earth! They captured Hubble and moved it to the space shuttle for repair. Soon it was able to take spectacular images of the universe.

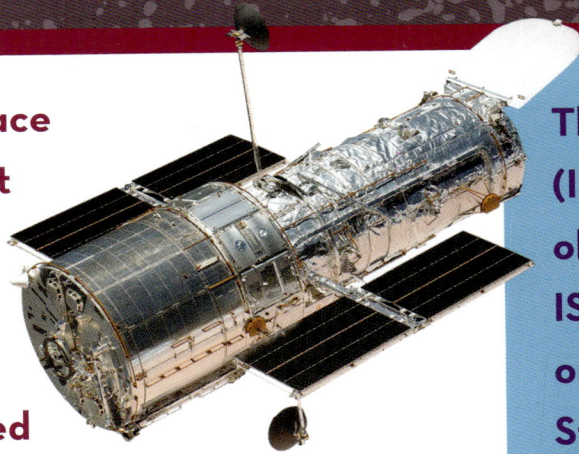

The Kepler Telescope was launched into space in 2009. It is a very powerful telescope. It can see a person on Earth turning off a porch light!

The International Space Station (ISS) is the largest, most complex object ever built in space. The ISS was put together in space one section at a time. The United States and Russia launched each piece separately. Astronaut crews joined the pieces together in orbit. The ISS took more than ten years and 30 missions to complete. It was completed in 2011.

▼

30 missions

Glossary

boosters (BOO-sturz) Boosters are rockets that launch spacecraft. Most boosters are not reusable.

foundation (fown-DAY-shuhn) A foundation is the base on which a building sits. Angkor Wat needs a strong foundation.

gladiators (GLAD-ee-ay-turz) Gladiators were warriors in ancient Rome who fought against other warriors or animals for public entertainment. Gladiators fought in the Colosseum.

groundwater (GROWND-wah-ter) Groundwater is water that is underground. The Angkor Wat moat kept the groundwater level steady.

orbited (OR-bit-uhd) To have orbited is to have followed an invisible path around a planet. The space shuttle orbited Earth.

pulleys (PUL-eez) Pulleys are wheels with ropes running through them that lift heavy loads. Ancient Egyptians did not have pulleys to lift heavy blocks.

reservoir (REZ-ur-vwar) A reservoir is a human-made lake that stores a large supply of water. The Three Gorges Dam created a large reservoir.

satellite (SAT-uh-lyt) A satellite is a machine that is sent into space to orbit a planet or moon. *Sputnik 1* was the first satellite.

space shuttle (SPAYSS SHUT-uhl) A space shuttle is a spacecraft that transports astronauts. The *Antonov AN-225* is big enough to carry a space shuttle.

theory (THEER-ee) A theory is an idea that has not been proven. It is a theory that Ancient Egyptians used sleds to move stone blocks.

thrust (THRUST) Thrust is the force from an aircraft or rocket engine. Rockets need thrust to get off the ground.

viaduct (VY-uh-duhkt) A viaduct is a long, high bridge that carries a road or railroad over a valley or street. The Millau Viaduct goes over the Tarn River valley.

To Learn More

In the Library

Hunt, Shannon. *Engineered!* Toronto, ON:
Kids Can Press, 2017.

Vorderman, Carol. *How to Be an Engineer.*
New York, NY: DK Publishing, 2018.

Woolf, Alex. *The Science of Buildings.*
New York, NY: Franklin Watts, 2019.

On the Web

Visit our website for links about engineering:

childsworld.com/links

*Note to Parents, Teachers, and Librarians: We routinely verify our Web links to make sure
they are safe and active sites. So encourage your readers to check them out!*

Index